G000126156

Real Men

Exploring together what a
Christian man thinks and does

14 sessions in Ephesians

Carl Laferton

With thanks to Tom C, Tom F, Jack and Tom D.

One2One Real Men
© The Good Book Company 2012

The Good Book Company
B1 Blenheim House, Blenheim Road
Epsom, Surrey KT19 9AP
Tel (UK): 0345 225 0880
Tel (US): 866 244 2165
Tel (int): +(44) 208 942 0880
email: admin@thegoodbook.co.uk

Websites:
UK & Europe: www.thegoodbook.co.uk
N America: www.thegoodbook.com
Australia: www.thegoodbook.com.au
New Zealand: www.thegoodbook.co.nz

ISBN: 9781908317605

Unless otherwise indicated, Scripture quotations in this publication are from The Holy Bible, New International Version, copyright © 1971, 1978, 1984 by International Bible Society. Used by permission. All rights reserved.

Printed in China

Introduction A real man

What is a man? When do you become a man? What are men supposed to do, anyway?

When Jesus walked on earth, He called men to follow Him. All sorts of men. Fishermen, soldiers, accountants, rich and poor, leaders and beggars.

He called them to come on an adventure, to turn their life into a challenge. He told the men He met to become real men—by following Him.

Your teenage years are a time when you stop being a child and start being a man. The question is: what does it mean to "start being a man"?

It's quite difficult to work that out. The society we live in has lots of suggestions. Your parents and your friends have ideas about what a real man thinks and does. Your school will tell you what it means to be mature.

But there's one person we often forget to listen to—and He's the one who made everything. Who made you. Who knows you inside out. Who wants what's best for you. Who made you to be a real man, and tells you how.

In the Bible, God has a lot to say about what a man is. He Himself lived on earth as a real man, Jesus. And the men who followed Jesus found out what it meant to be real men by getting to know Him. It's exactly the same today.

Are you ready to find out what it takes?

contents

Living the adventure

One of Jesus' first followers was a guy called Paul. His life as a follower of Jesus in the first century saw him standing up to the might of the Roman Empire, travelling thousands of miles, causing riots, being imprisoned and making daring escapes. His life was full of adventures! But each one was part of a bigger adventure—the adventure of living as a Christian, wherever Jesus takes you, whatever He asks you to do.

Christian-hater to Christian leader
Paul wasn't brought up a Christian. In fact, he became a fierce enemy of Christianity, and after Jesus had risen and gone back to heaven, Paul tried to imprison and execute Jesus' friends. Until, that is, he was walking along a road and Jesus appeared to him in a blinding light (you can read about it in Acts 9 v 1-19).

Unsurprisingly, he changed his mind about Jesus after that and spent the rest of his life talking about Him, rather than torturing His people.

Wherever Paul went, he told people about Jesus. Most places he went, the majority dismissed his message—but some became Christians. And so by the time Paul left, there was a church in that city.

Paul and Ephesus
One of these churches was in a city called Ephesus, which is in what we now call Turkey. Paul spent a couple of years leading that church, before moving on.

Later, he wrote a letter to them, reminding them what followers of Jesus know to be true about God and themselves, and explaining to them how to follow Jesus in their everyday lives; how to be real men (and women, and children). Just like the rest of the Bible, these words were written by a man, but inspired by God. They're Paul's words—but they're also God's words.

And it's this letter, which is called "Ephesians", which you're going to be digging in to over the next couple of months...

How this booklet works

In here you'll find 14 sessions, each looking at a bit of Ephesians.

Seven sessions (the odd-numbered ones) are JOINT, for you to do with an older Christian guy—just the two of you (or you and a friend and him). The other seven (the even-numbered ones) are SOLO, for you to do on your own in your own time. So it'll take you seven weeks to do the whole booklet if you meet up weekly, 14 if you meet up every two weeks. When you get together, it'll probably take you 45 minutes to do the session. On your own, the sessions should take around half an hour at the most.

Lots of people find it helpful to write down answers to some, or all, of the questions—it helps you focus on the question, and remember what you found in the Bible. So there are spaces left to scribble something down. But if the thought of having to write stuff down makes you want to close this book, then don't feel you have to!

You may well have been given this booklet by an older man at your church who leads your youth group, or by your dad; they'll be hoping you can both learn together more about how to be a real man. Maybe you've found this booklet yourself... if you have, you'll get most out of it if you do it with an older guy who's been a Christian for at least a few years. So try to find one at a church or Christian youth group near you.

It doesn't matter whether you're a follower of Jesus, or someone who wants to find out about Him and what He says. And because this is a booklet for men, it doesn't pull punches or tiptoe round the issues we might find difficult. That's not how real men deal with things.

The Bible quotes in this booklet are from the NIV 1984 (New International Version). If you have, or can get your hands on, that translation, then do—but the sessions will work with Bible versions like the ESV, the NASB, and the NIrV (and probably lots of others!) too.

If you're an older man, wanting to use this booklet with a teenager, you'll find a helpful online guide at www.thegoodbook.co.uk/Realmenguide, which is well worth looking at before you start.

You're a man in a plan

Today's Bible section: **Ephesians chapter 1, verses 1-14**

A TO START OFF

❶ Describe who you are in three sentences.

B LETT-ERS BEGIN   Read Ephesians 1 v 1-2

These days, you start a letter by saying who it's to, and finish it with who it's from. In Paul's day, they started by saying who it was from and who it was to, and then got on with it.

❷ Who is this letter from, and who is it to (v 1)?

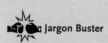 **Jargon Buster**
Apostle = the men God chose to write the New Testament and to set up His church.
Saints = "distinctive people". It's a word Paul often used to describe Christians, because they live differently to others.

C GOD'S PLAN   Read verses 3-14

❸ Paul repeats one phrase loads of times here—it's the last two words of verse 3. Write down the phrase.. Then each time you find that phrase, read out that sentence and its verse number.

Just to be awkward, sometimes the phrase finishes with "him" instead of "Christ". You should spot it eight times!

This phrase is a wonderful way to describe what a "Christian" actually is. It's someone who is united to Jesus—who knows Him as a friend. If we are "in Christ", He shares everything He has with us. Wow!

4 When did God make His plan to choose people to be "in him" (v 4)? Why is this amazing?

5 When Paul says "through his blood" in verse 7, he's thinking of when Jesus died on the cross. Use the jargon buster to work out what God did by sending Jesus to die on the cross.

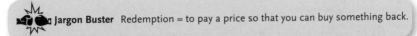 **Jargon Buster**   Redemption = to pay a price so that you can buy something back.

6 Look at verse 13. What does God give people when they believe the good news about Jesus (the "gospel")?

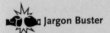 **Jargon Buster**   Holy Spirit = God. God is one God, in three persons, each different but fully God—Father, Son and Holy Spirit (which is what people mean when they talk about the Trinity).

A deposit is something you give which guarantees that you'll give something even better later. For a school trip, you might pay a 10% deposit as a way of showing you'll definitely pay the other 90% six months later.

7 So what is Paul telling us about the Holy Spirit (v 14)?

8 In verse 10, "when the times will have reached their fulfilment" means the day that God reaches the end of His plan. Who is going to be recognised as ruler of absolutely everything?

9 At the bottom of this page is a "timeline". Can you fill in the parts of God's plan that you've been looking at?

10 But why did God bother with this massive eternal plan?! Why did He choose to make people part of His plan?! Find the almost identical phrase that crops up in v 6, v 12 and v 14. That's the reason! What do you think it means?

D THINK ABOUT IT

11 At the beginning you had to describe yourself in three sentences. Using the timeline to help you, how would Paul describe a Christian man in three sentences?
A Christian man is someone who...

12 Imagine you were one of the people Paul wrote this to. How would Paul's words make you feel as a Christian?

13 Have these verses changed the way you think about the Christian life? If yes, how?

Before time

←– – – – – – – – – ––––––––––––––––––––
　　　　　　　　　　 ○　　　　　　　　　　　　　　　 ○
　　　　　　　　 Creation　　　　　　　　　　　　　 Cross

PRAYER TIME

Come up with a one-sentence prayer thanking God for something (or lots of things!) you've learned from this section:

MEMORY VERSE

"He chose us IN HIM before the creation of the world."
Ephesians 1 v 4

Now   Jesus returns

Man's biggest problem

Today's Bible section: Ephesians chapter 2, verses 1-3

God sent Jesus to die so people could "have redemption" (chapter 1 verse 7). He bought us back so we could be part of God's amazing plan. It cost Jesus, God's Son, His life. But why does God need to buy us back? What do we need buying back from?

That's what this Bible study is all about, as we look at "Man's biggest problem".

If you're struggling to work out the answer to one of the questions below, it's probably the question's fault rather than your fault! Have a stab at it, put a **?** next to it and when you meet up next week make sure you ask about it.

Before you start, pray that God would help you understand what He's telling you in these verses.

A THE DOC'S DIAGNOSIS

❶ What would you say is your biggest problem in life at the moment?

When you're ill, you go to the doctor. He works out what's wrong with you (the diagnosis), and gives you something to make you better (the cure).

❷ Why do you need the diagnosis before you get the cure?

In this section, Paul wants us to see there's something wrong with us. He gives us a diagnosis, and it's not nice to hear. The good news is there's a cure, which you'll find out about in Session Three.
But for now, **read Ephesians 2 verses 1-3.**

❸ How would you decide whether someone is alive or dead?

❹ In verse 1, Paul's talking to followers of Christ. How does he describe what they used to be before they became Christians?

That's pretty weird! Paul's telling these Christians that they were "dead"—even though they were walking and talking humans. That's because the Bible doesn't think of life as having a beating heart, breathing lungs and a brain that thinks. And it doesn't think of death as being buried because your heart and lungs and brain have stopped working. The Bible thinks of "life" as knowing the God who gives life, and "death" as being separated from God.

So someone can be walking around, talking to people, having fun, feeling alive, but actually they are "dead"—separated from God.

❺ What is it that makes people "dead" (v 1)?

Verses 2-3 say that all of us decide that, when it comes to how we should think, speak and act, we don't listen to or obey the God who made us. We decide other people know better than Him, or the devil knows better than Him, or simply that we know better than Him.

That's what *sin* is—being disobedient to God, living our way instead of God's way.

❻ So, like everyone else, "we were by nature..." what (end of v 3)?

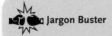
Jargon Buster   Objects of... = things (or people) who receive...
Wrath = deserved anger. Here, it's talking about God's anger.

7 What is the Bible's diagnosis of the problem every single man on earth has?

8 Why is this the most serious problem any man can face (think about your answer to Question Five)?

9 Do you (or any man or woman) deserve to be part of God's plan, which we found out about in the last session? Why, or why not?

D SUM IT UP

10 One thing I've found out or been reminded about God is...

One thing I've found out or been reminded about myself is...

If you've got any questions about what you've read, scribble them here...

PRAYER TIME

You might be in the habit of talking to God, or you may never have done it before. It's a great thing to do, and you don't have to use special words or long sentences. Here are some things you might like to say to Him about what He's said to you in this Bible section:

- Thank God that in the Bible He tells it straight.
- Talk to God about ways in which you've disobeyed Him in the last week.
- In the next session, we'll see that God has made a way for people to be "made ... alive" (v 5). Thank Him now that He hasn't left us to face His anger. Thank Him for giving us a way out.

The Man's solution Joint

Today's Bible section: Ephesians 2 v 4-10

A GETTING STARTED

1 Sum up in a sentence what you found out in 2 v 1-3 about the problem that every man faces.

2 What do we deserve from God?

Lots of people think that God is like Santa Claus (except that He's real!). Santa, the story goes, gives presents to children if they've been good, but he doesn't give anything to children who've been selfish or nasty.

Perhaps God's like that in real life; if you're good, He gives you eternal life, but if not, then you miss out.

What we're going to read here blows that idea away...

B A BIG BUT! **Read Ephesians 2 v 4-10**

3 Remember the diagnosis of verses 1-3. Why is the very first word of verse 4 such good news?

4 What has God done for people who are "with Christ"?
• verse 5:

• verse 6:

5 So, someone who is "with Christ" (a Christian) now has a seat reserved (v 6). Where? How does that make you feel?

6 Why did God "save" us in this way (v 4)?

C THE "G" WORDS

7 Paul uses a Bible jargon word to describe how we are "saved" (changed from dead to alive). It's in verse 5 and verse 8. What is it?

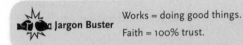 **Jargon Buster** G.......................... = showing kindness to someone who doesn't deserve it.

8 If that's how we're saved, then how are people *not* saved (v 8-9)?

Jargon Buster Works = doing good things.
Faith = 100% trust.

9 Apart from "grace", there's another word in verse 8 which describes what God offers us in Jesus Christ, also beginning with "g"—what is it?

Let's think about this—do you have to earn a gift?

Why might someone give you a gift (think about someone giving you a birthday present)?

When someone offers you a gift, what do you have to do to make it yours?

10 With Santa, the idea is that he gives out his presents on the basis of what people have done. How is God's gift different to that?

Imagine that someone said to you: "How can you be sure you're going to heaven?" Use this passage to help you think about what you might say.

"I know I'm going to heaven because God...

"

"Getting to heaven is not about...

"

God offers us a place in heaven with Christ, but we have to decide whether to take it or not.

Have you accepted His gift of His Son, Jesus Christ, and said "thank you"?

Are you looking forward to life with God, or are you still facing His anger (v 3)?

Whether or not to accept the gift of Jesus Christ is the **most important decision** you'll ever make.

Ask yourself: "Have I accepted God's undeserved gift of new life in Jesus, so that I don't need to face His anger?"

E ONE MORE THING

This is all great... and verse 10 adds something else.

11 What do people who are "in Christ Jesus" now do with their lives? Why is this exciting?

F THINK ABOUT IT

12 Why is God's grace brilliant?

⑬ Why is the decision whether or not to accept God's gift the most important one you'll ever make?

⑭ God gives His followers "good works" to do (v 10). They don't do them *to be* saved by God, but because God has *already* saved them. What might that mean for you and the way you live, do you think?

PRAYER TIME

From this bit of the Bible:
I'm giving thanks to God for... (an encouragement):

I want to ask God for help with... (a challenge):

MEMORY VERSE

"It is by GRACE you have been saved, through faith."
Ephesians 2 v 8

Today's Bible section: Ephesians 3 v 14-21

> So far in this letter from Paul to the Christians in Ephesus, we've discovered that:
> - God's got an amazing plan which involves men and women and is all about Jesus.
> - Because we disobey God, we're facing His anger.
> - Because of God's grace, we can accept His gift of Jesus, and be part of His plan.
>
> Now, we're going to start asking the question—what difference does being a Christian, a man who's part of God's plan, make to your life?

Before you start, take a few moments to speak to God. Thank Him for giving you His word, the Bible. Ask Him to help you understand what you're looking at. And ask Him to enable you to follow Jesus better as a result.

Now open up your Bible and **read Ephesians 3 v 14-21.**

A ON HIS KNEES

1 What's Paul doing in this section? (The first two words of verse 16 should help you out!)

2 Skip down to verse 20. What does Paul know about God which means that it's worth praying to Him?

B WHAT WE NEED

3 What does Paul say is at work inside a Christian (v20)?

P

All men would love to have lots of this—maybe as a general who can command huge armies, or as a sports star who keeps us glued to the TV when they're playing. Paul says that whoever they are, and wherever they are, Christian men have inside them a power much greater than any general or celebrity—the power of God, which is greater than we can even begin to imagine.

And if you're a Christian, it's inside you right now. Amazing!

But what do we need God to do with His power? Paul's prayer tells us we need Him to do two things...

C POWER PART ONE

❹ Read the sentence that starts halfway through verse 17 with "And I pray that..." Paul is asking God to give his Christian friends the power to do what (the answer is in verse 18)?

Verse 19 tells us that Jesus' love "surpasses knowledge"—which means we can never know everything about Christ's love for us. And so we need God's power to enable us to even begin to understand the amazing-ness of Christ's love in coming and dying to buy us back. To redeem us. To change us from dead to alive. To make us part of God's plan.

D POWER PART TWO

❺ Read the sentence that starts at the beginning of verse 16. Paul is praying for His friends. What does he ask God to use His power to do for them (look at the beginning of verse 17)?

This part's a bit complicated, but it's also very exciting... As soon as someone puts their faith in Christ, they're given the Holy Spirit as a guarantee that they will have eternal life (remember 1 v 13-14?). Christ lives in them through the Holy Spirit.

Here, in 3 v 16-17, Paul's asking God to make his Christian friends people who Christ doesn't just live in, but makes a home in.

It's kind of like the difference between squatting in a house, and owning one. Squatters live in a house, but it's not theirs, it's got someone else's stuff in it, and it's not decorated as they'd like.

But when you own a house, it's yours. It's got your furniture and your decorations, just as you want it.

So it is with the heart of a Christian. Christ lives there already—but God wants to change that heart to make it a home for Jesus. He wants Christians to get rid of the rubbish stuff, sin, left over from when they were disobeying God, and He wants their hearts to be places that are just as Jesus wants them.

Christians can't do that on their own. They need God's help. They need God's power to change them. *And that's what Paul's praying here—for God's powerful Spirit to make their hearts more and more a place where Jesus is at home.*

6 Paul's asking for big things here. Can God do them (v 20-21)?

E **THINK ABOUT IT**

7 Why should this section encourage us to pray for ourselves and our friends about all sorts of things?

8 What kind of things does Paul show us we should be praying for our Christian friends, and for ourselves?

PRAYER TIME

HOW? Christian guys will want to speak to God regularly... but often it's hard to get started, and keep going! Here are six key tips...

Do it daily: Aim to speak to God every day.

Set a time: Work out when's a good time for you to pray each day. If you make it a habit (like brushing your teeth when you get up) it's much easier. Good times might be getting up five minutes earlier, or when you get in from school, or straight after dinner. By the way, trying to do it when you get into bed is usually not a great idea—people often fall asleep!

Start small: Don't worry about praying for a long time if you're new to it. But at the same time, try to build up your prayers over a few weeks. The more you do it, the easier it'll get!

Use STOP: It's often hard to work out what to say to God! This four-part prayer is one you can use really easily to help you speak to God about your life, your worries, your failings and successes.

Sorry for...
Thank you for...
Others I'd like to pray for...
Please help me with...

Write it down: Jotting down what you want to say before you say it to God can help if you struggle to know what to say. It also gives you a written record of what you've prayed, so you can look back at it and see how God has answered your prayers.

Get on with it: Don't just think you ought to do it. Don't try, find it a bit difficult, and give up. Be a real man. Do it!

NOW! Use your answers to Question Eight to scribble a prayer down here. Then say it to the God who can do more than you can even imagine!

Session 5   A man in church   Joint

Today's Bible section: Ephesians 4 v 1-13

A   GETTING STARTED

❶ How can you tell that someone is a Christian?

B   A VITAL VERSE   Read Ephesians 4 v 1

❷ What does Paul urge these Christians to do (v 1)?

❸ What have they been "called" to be? (Look back to 1 v 4 and the start of verse 6 to see what God has chosen Christians to be, and to do.)

Ephesians 4 v 1 is a crucial verse. Last week we learned that it's by grace—God's undeserved kindness to us in Jesus Christ—that we can have eternal life and be part of God's plan. That's what we've been "called" to have and enjoy.

And now Paul is going to tell us how a man who is part of God's plan should try to live, so that God gets praise.

C   HOW TO DO CHURCH   Read verses 2-13

In these verses, Paul is telling Christians how to relate to one another as they meet together—at church.

❹ How does Paul describe the church (v 12)?

Paul uses the word "one" seven times in verses 4-6! He's making the point that the Christians in the church must be "one body". Because they are united ("one") in their faith in Jesus, they should be united and work together.

5 So, what should Christians be making "every effort to do" (v 3)?

A sports team is much stronger if everyone is united, working together. So is a body of Christians—a church. How can a church be united?

D **UNITED: TIP ONE**

6 How should we treat others at our church (v 2)? Why is this sometimes difficult?

Christians can work for a united church by...

E **UNITED: TIP TWO**

7 What has Christ given (v 7)? Who has He given it to?

We found out in session two that "grace" means undeserved kindness. Here, Paul is talking about Christ making us good at things. God, in His undeserved kindness, gives all Christians eternal life; He also gives all Christians abilities and talents. So although a church should be united, the people in it will be different from each other.

8 What should all God's people be using their gifts to do (v 12)?

9 What will happen to a church where everyone's doing this (end of v 12 - beginning of v 13)?

Christians can work for a united church by...

Paul could have begun his section of Ephesians about living a life worthy of the calling you have received by talking about the things men tend to care most about—relationships, work, sex, marriage, family. And he's going to talk about all that stuff later on! But he chooses to start by talking about the church.

10 What does this tell us about the importance of church in the life of a Christian man?

F THINK ABOUT YOU

11 How should *you* treat people who are also part of the church (v 2)?

12 Who has given you the gifts or talents that you have (v 7)? Why (v 12)? What might verse 12 look like in your life?

SCENARIOS

Sam enjoys church. He can see his friends and the talks are good. A schoolfriend has asked him to play in his football team on Sunday mornings—now he needs to choose between that and going to church. It won't matter if he misses church—he can read his Bible at home, and no one will miss him much. *What does this Bible section say to Sam?*

Dave is a seriously good piano player. He's in a jazz band and is doing Grade 8. The minister asked him to play for the church, but he said no. He doesn't really like the tunes he'd have to play, plus he's so busy practising for concerts and his music exam that he doesn't have time to play the piano at church as well. *What does this Bible section say to Dave (think about v 7 and v 12)?*

Joe likes going to church on a Sunday—there's a group for teenagers his age. Afterwards he spends his time with them. Some of the older people are a bit boring and they ask him silly questions, so he avoids them. The younger children want him to play with them, but he's too grown up for all that now. *What does this Bible section say to Joe (think about v 2-3)?*

MEMORY VERSE

"LIVE A LIFE WORTHY of the calling you have received."   *Ephesians 4 v 1*

PRAYER TIME

Thank God for your church. Think of some specific things about it to say thank you for.

Ask God to help you be a helpful member of the body. Think of some specific things you want God to help you with.

G BUT WHAT CAN I DO?

It's easy to think that there's nothing that you can contribute to your church; but verse 7 says: "to EACH ONE OF US grace has been given". So Jesus has given you something you can use to serve the other Christians at your church!

Firstly, simply turn up! It really encourages older people to see teenagers in church! Then, think about whether Jesus has made you able to do these things for the people at your church...

- *Smile at people*
- *Chat to people who don't have other people to talk to, before or after the service*
- *Encourage people to keep going as Christians*
- *Read the Bible or lead the prayers during a service*
- *Play a musical instrument*
- *Clean and tidy*
- *Helping with food and drinks*
- *Lead a Bible study group*
- *Give some money*
- *Help with a kids' club*
- *Invite friends*
- *Something else I know I could do is...*

A grown-up man Solo

Today's Bible section: Ephesians 4 v 14-16

A NEED SOME BODY

❶ In one minute, write down every part of a body that's needed for it to work well:

Now take a moment to pray to God, thanking Him that He's written this bit of His word to help you. Ask Him to help you understand it and enable you to live the life He wants you to. And remember to answer in your own words!

❷ Sum up in a sentence or two what you learned from the last Bible session (4 v 1-13; read it through quickly if you can't remember!).

The verses we're looking at now are part of that same section, about the church or "body of Christ".

B HAVEN'T YOU GROWN?!　　　　**Read Ephesians 4 v 14-16**

❸ How does this body grow (v 15)?

❹ Think back to the last Bible section—what are the "parts" of the body of Christ (or to put it another way, what is the body of Christ made up of)? And how does each "part" do its "work"?

And the head of this body is Jesus Christ (v 15). It's His church, and He should be in charge of it!

5 Look at the beginning of verse 15. How can we "grow up" as Christians and become more and more like Christ?

Let's take a silly example to think through what this means...
It's very hot, and you've been playing tennis; now you're going out to meet some friends. As you leave, your sister notices you've got a really big sweat patch on your back from the tennis.
Match up the responses with which attitude they represent:

"Have a great time, bro!" (I'd better not say anything, I love him and don't want him to be upset. Best not to tell him about the sweat patch, or he might be embarrassed.)	"Bro, you've got a bit of a sweat patch on your back. You probably haven't noticed. If I were you, I'd go and get changed before you go and meet your mates."	"Haha, you've got a huge sweat patch—can't believe you didn't notice! I'd never make that mistake. You look ridiculous—I'm going to text my mates now and tell them you nearly went out like that!"
SPEAKING THE TRUTH IN LOVE	**Speaking the truth, but not with love**	**Speaking with love, but not the truth**

That's a silly example—but in church, Paul tells us all to speak the truth in love. That means we need to be honest with people if we can see they're doing something wrong. We need to tell the truth; but we also need to be loving with people and tell them as gently and helpfully as we can.

SCENARIO

Your friend from church hasn't been for a while, nor has he been to youth group. You know it's because he has some new friends and hangs around with them instead. You know he's really happy to have new friends because he's been quite lonely at his school. *How would you speak the truth in love to him?*

C GROW UP!

People often complain about teenagers "needing to be mature" (often when you've done something "immature"). Maturing is something that happens as you grow older (all of us are always maturing, even elderly people!). And maturing is something that's good to do as a Christian, too. No one wants to stay a baby for ever, and it's not good to stay a baby Christian for ever either!

6 What can happen to "baby" Christians (v 14)? Put this in your own words?

It's by maturing as Christian men that we can make sure this doesn't happen to us. We mature as Christian men **as part of our church**, not on our own. And we mature as we are truthful and loving with others (even when that's hard) and as others are truthful and loving with us (even when that's hard too!)

D THINK ABOUT IT

7 Why do you need to go to church?

8 Why do others at church rely on you to use your gifts at church, and to "speak the truth in love" (think about the church being like a "body")?

9 Is there anyone at the moment who you need to encourage to start coming to church, either because they've stopped coming recently or because they say they are a Christian but never come to church? What could you say to them?

❿ One encouragement from this Bible section is...

One challenge from this Bible section is...

PRAYER TIME

Use your answers to Question Ten to speak to God now (remember, it often helps to write down first what you want to say).

A man who is different

Today's Bible section: Ephesians 4 v 17-28

A FASHION PARADE

❶ What's your favourite item of clothing?

❷ Can you think of something you've worn in the past (maybe someone else got it for you?!) which you can't believe you ever wore because it's just so awful?!

B OLD SELF, NEW SELF   **Read Ephesians 4 v 17-24**

This section is all about something Christians used to wear, but now want to take off (v 22), and something that Christians now love to put on (v 24).

❸ How does v 22 describe the "old self"? How does verse 24 describe the "new self"?

❹ Are Christian men going to be similar or different to guys around them who aren't Christians?

❺ Is this easy? Why, or why not?

Sometimes it's easy to think that it doesn't really matter, that perhaps we can wear our old self and our new self at the same time or just swap them around. Maybe that's why Paul describes what the "old self" is like in more detail in verse 17-19...

C NOT GOOD Re-read verses 17-19

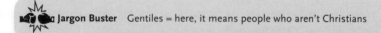

Jargon Buster   Gentiles = here, it means people who aren't Christians

6 What's the biggest problem with being a "Gentile" (v 18)?

Paul says this leads to losing your sense of right and wrong ("sensi-tivity", v 19), which means you just do what feels good ("sensuality"), and so you end up doing loads of stuff which God says is wrong ("impurity").

7 Can living like this ever leave you totally satisfied (end of v 19)? Can you think of examples of this, perhaps in your own life?

8 What strikes you about how Paul describes a "Gentile", or "not-Christian", lifestyle?

D BE RE-MINDED Re-read verses 22-24

It's not always easy to take off our old, self-centred self and put on our new, Christ-obeying self. Paul says it all starts with how we think (v 23).

9 How can we be "made new in the attitude of our minds"? There's a repeated word in v 21 and 22 which holds the key. What is it? What is Paul reminding us we need?

COMPARE AND CONTRAST   Read verses 25-28

❿ Here are some contrasts between what our old self wants to do, and what our new Christian self should do:

	Old self	New self	Why?
v 25			
v 26-7			
v 28			

On pages 64 and 65 you'll find two "selfs", shaped as shirts—one old self, and one new self. Over the next few sessions, as we find out more about the differences between our old self and our new self, you can write them on these shirts. Why not start now with these three?

F **THINK ABOUT IT**

⓫ In which areas of your life do you find it hardest to be a man who is different to people who aren't Christians? What can you remember from this passage next time you're in that situation?

SCENARIOS

Tommy is finding being a Christian a real struggle. When he refuses to do things his friends at school do, they just laugh at him and say that surely God would want him to enjoy himself. Tommy is determined to keep going as a Christian, but he thinks that sometimes it's a good idea to tag along with his friends, just so they don't think he's different and strange? *How would you help Tommy... from v 22-24?   ...from v 17-19?*

Ryan is getting a bit bored of Bible study and talks at church. He knows that Jesus died for him and has saved him, he understands that eternal life is God's gift of undeserved kindness to him... so why does he need to bother listening anymore? *There are lots of things we could say to Ryan, but use v 20-24 to tell Ryan if he's right or not, and why.*

PRAYER TIME

One encouragement to give thanks for:

One challenge to pray about:

MEMORY VERSE

"Put on the NEW SELF, created to be like God."
Ephesians 4 v 24

Today's Bible section: Ephesians 4 v 29-32

The average guy says 7,000 words every day. That's 2,548,000 a year—quite a lot (don't try to count them). And a survey made the amazing discovery that our favourite topic of conversation is... wait for it... girls. Who'd have guessed that?!

Have you ever thought about how you use your 2 million words each year? We use words for all sorts of things – to tell people good news and bad news, to cheer people up and make them laugh, to prove we're right or admit we're wrong.

You'll remember from the last Bible section we did that guys who follow Christ are to act differently from those around them. We saw three ways to do that in the last section (can you remember what they were? If not, have a look at your "new self" on page 66).

In this session, we're going to think about one way which will make a HUGE difference to us.

But before we do, don't forget to pray that God would help you not only understand what He's saying, but help you let it make a difference to how you live your life.

A CHOOSE YOUR WORDS   **Read Ephesians 4 v 29-32**

We'll mostly be looking at verse 29...

❶ What should a Christian guy *not* do?

❷ Write a quick list of the kind of stuff that you think "unwholesome talk" means.

❸ What did you write down—maybe nasty teasing, shouting, gossiping, swearing, dirty jokes? Why is it hard not to do these things?

4 So that's what we *shouldn't* use our 7,000 words a day for. What *should* we be saying (v 29)?

This doesn't *only* mean saying nice things to and about others. It also means encouraging Christians to keep following Jesus. That's really challenging! It's hard to stop letting ourselves say anything unwholesome, but it's even more difficult to use what we say to encourage and build others up! If you're going to do this, you'll have to make a deliberate effort.

5 What difference would it make to those around you if everything you said built people up?

Don't forget to add what verses 29 and 31-32 say to your "old self" and "new self" on pages 64-65. While you're at it, if you look at verse 30, you'll see that men who follow Christ should not grieve the Holy Spirit (by not being united—remember back in 4 v 3 we were told to "keep the unity of the Spirit"). You can add that on too!

B THINK BEFORE YOU SPEAK

Here are some helpful questions to think about before we open our mouths, so we can be men who obey verse 29:

"Is this unwholesome? Could it upset someone? Is it something I'd like Jesus to hear me saying?"

"Will this build up the person I'm talking to? (Am I being positive instead of negative? Am I trying to encourage this person to follow Jesus?)"

"Is what I'm saying going to benefit the people who are listening, or am I really only saying it to benefit me by making me look cool, or funny, or clever?"

6 Think of some specific ways you need to work at "benefiting those who listen", and at cutting out "unwholesome talk":

7 If you become known as someone who follows verse 29, how will that affect the way your non-Christian friends view your Christian faith?

8 Emails, texts and social networking sites like Facebook and Google+ weren't around when Paul was writing. But how does verse 29 guide us in the way we use these things as Christians?

You'll probably say 7,000 words tomorrow. You may well type a load, too. The big question is—how will you use those words? Will people see from what you say, and don't say, that you are different—that you are a man who follows Christ?

PRAYER TIME

Thank God that He speaks to you in the Bible. Thank God that you can have good conversations with others every day.

Tell God about the things that have challenged you from verse 29, and ask for His help.

Is there a particular situation where you know it'll be hard to obey verse 29? Speak to God about it now.

And if you hadn't already prayed today, why not carry on praying about other things now? Use STOP (see page 23) to help you if you'd find it useful.

A man who loves right

Today's Bible section: Ephesians 5 v 1-14

Two things to say about this section. First, it's about some issues that might be very personal to you, and you might not want to talk about them. That's fine! Feel free to say "I don't want to talk about this", and think about the question in your head instead.

Second, we're going to work backwards through this section.

A **LIGHT, DARK AND FRUIT** **Read Ephesians 5 v 8-14**

❶ Draw a picture describing what Paul's saying in verse 8 (or, if you really don't like drawing, just sum it up in your own words!).

❷ Let's just remind ourselves of what we saw in Session Three (ages ago now!)—how is it that we get eternal life in Christ, or pass from "darkness" to "light" (have a look at 2 v 4-8)?

❸ If we're "light in the Lord" now, what should we do (v 9-10)?

Today, Paul's going to tell us how to live "in the light" in the area of life which guys think about most, talk about most, worry about most and get wrong most—love and sex.

B **OUT OF BOUNDS** **Read verses 3-7**

❹ What does Paul say is "out of bounds" for men who follow Christ (what he calls "holy people")? Fill in the table...

	What's out of bounds?	What does this look like in real life?
v 3 (a)		
v 3 (b)		
v 3 (c)		
v 4 (a)		
v 4 (b)		
v 4 (c)		

5 Which do you most struggle with?

6 Why does Paul write verses 5-6 here, do you think?
Does this mean that anyone who gets things wrong with sex can't be forgiven? (If you need to, look back to 2 v 3-5 to help.)

C NOT JUST A LIST OF DON'TS

Those are the negatives—Paul gives us THREE positive things to do too:

7 When Christian men think and talk about sex, what should they be doing (end of v 4)? Why?

1

Paul tells us in verse 11 to "have nothing to do with the fruitless deeds of darkness, but rather expose them". Christian men, when they're with other men, should be so different in the area of sex and love and relationships that simply by acting and speaking differently they "expose" others' behaviour as selfish and wrong. That needs COURAGE.

2

Read verses 1-2

8 Whose love is Paul talking about in verse 2? How did He show how much He loves us?

9 How are we to react to this type of love (v 1)?

10 There are two types of "love". Both begin with a "g":

Verse 2: Jesus' love G

Verse 3: Immoral love is G   y

Everyone loves in one way or the other. We can love ourselves, and use our sex lives to get what we can from others—that's *greed*. Or we can love others, and want to *give* what we can, doing what's best for others, just as Jesus did. The world around us says: "Do *greedy* love". Christian men try to do *giving* love.

D   THINK ABOUT IT

11 What temptations are you going to face in the next five years in this area of life? What will make them hard to resist?

12 When we get things wrong, what do we need to remember about how we're saved (look back to 2 v 8-9)?

13 One thing I need to change in my thinking or the way I live is...

Write a prayer paragraph based on what you've found out from this Bible section:

SCENARIOS

Mike and his mates are well into girls. Mike's not actually going to go out with anyone till he knows that it's right and it's someone he gets along really well with. But he loves talking about girls with his mates, having a laugh about what they'd like to do with them and rating them as to who's the fittest. *What does Mike need to learn from this section?*

Joel and his girlfriend Sarah have been together for two years. They know God wants them to leave having sex till they're married. But there's loads of other good stuff they can do in bed which isn't really sex. And Joel likes being "normal" with his friends by being able to talk about what he and Sarah do together, even though they don't go the whole way. *From this Bible section, how would you encourage and/or challenge Joel?*

Matt really loves his girlfriend and she loves him, so they've decided to have sex. It just feels right to both of them, so how can there be a problem? They even prayed about their decision and it still feels right, so they're going to go for it. *What would you want to say to Matt?*

MEMORY VERSE

"Live a life of LOVE, just as Christ loved us and GAVE himself up for us."   *Ephesians 5 v 2*

A man who lives right

Today's Bible section: Ephesians 5 v 15-20

Before you begin, pray that God would enable you to understand the passage and that it would make a big difference to your life.

A DRINKING HABITS

❶ Let's be honest: What do you think people (and maybe you) enjoy about getting drunk? And what would you say is bad about it?

B TWO DO'S   Read Ephesians 5 v 15-17

❷ What does Paul tell us to be in verse 15?

a: **C**

b: **W**

❸ Why (end v 16)?

It's easy not to think much about how we live. We just get on with it! But Paul tells us to be careful—to concentrate on how we act—and to be "wise", which means to "understand what the Lord's will is". The Bible says that's true wisdom; not being really great at school or college, but knowing how God wants you to live, and getting on with it.

C A WAY TO BE WISE

Here's an example of something that seems like a great idea to most people, but which, if we "understand what the Lord's will is", we'll realise is rubbish compared to living God's way. **Read verses 18-20.**

❹ What does Paul tell us not to do (v 18)?

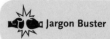

Jargon Buster Debauchery = taking great pleasure in immoral behaviour (especially sexual immorality).

Getting drunk leads to our judgement not being as good as usual. So instead of being able to "understand what the Lord's will is", we'll end up doing things we'd never do if we were sober.

5 Why would it be easier to ignore in our lives what Paul's saying here?

6 What should Christian men do instead (v 18)?

The big question is: what do you want to be under the influence of? Booze, which makes you behave not like your new self and do things you wouldn't normally want to do... or... the Holy Spirit, who helps you behave like the man God's created you to be?

7 What do men who are "filled with the Spirit" do?

a (v 19):

Have you ever heard drunk people singing? It's usually awful and makes no sense! But people who are under the influence of the Holy Spirit sing too. They sing to encourage each other and to tell God how they feel about Him—a much better type of singing than drunken singing!

b (v 20):

Why can men who follow Christ (who say "no" to the world's ideas and "yes" to the Holy Spirit) be "always giving thanks"? Because men who are filled with the Spirit know that this is the way real men live—enjoying life under the influence of His Spirit. It's the way people who Jesus died for live, the way God created them to live.

People tend to encourage getting drunk as a bit of a laugh and a great adventure—but real satisfaction, and the real adventure, lie in following Christ and being part of God's eternal plan. If you get drunk, you can't remember the night before: if you are filled with the Spirit, you know that God chose you even before the creation of the world.

D THINK ABOUT IT

Being filled with alcohol means we lose our usual sense of perspective and judgement.
Being filled with the Spirit means we will be careful and wise in making judgements.

Perhaps the next time it would be easy to get drunk with your friends (which may be next year, or may be next weekend), it's worth asking: "What do I want to be under the influence of this evening—alcohol, or the Holy Spirit?"

E SOME TIPS

Maybe, having read these verses, you know you need to change the way you've been drinking and behaving. But *knowing* and *doing* are two very different things! Here are some practical tips you might find helpful:

• Work out beforehand what you'll say if someone asks you why you're not getting drunk. Maybe something like: "I'm a Christian, and I know God doesn't want me to get drunk. And actually, I'll have a much better time if I don't!"

• Remember that God wants men who follow Him to stick to the law of their country (if you've got time, look up Romans 13 v 1). So make sure you know what the laws are about where and when it's legal to drink alcohol. That doesn't mean that if it's legal, you should drink... but it does mean that if it's illegal, then you shouldn't!

• Decide before you go out how much you are going to drink. Then stick to it.

• Ask a Christian friend to do two things for you:
    pray about it.
    ask you each week or each month how you've been doing.

• And if you need to, just give up drinking alcohol altogether. Better to have nothing to drink, than to have too much.

PRAYER TIME

One encouragement to give thanks to God for:

One challenge from this Bible section to pray to God about:

A man and his wife

Today's Bible section: Ephesians 5 v 21-33

> In this section, Paul talks about marriage. He wants us to see what kind of a husband a Christian man should be. OK, so you're not married now—but the chances are you will be one day! And, as the Scouts say, it's good to "be prepared".
>
> Marriage used to be seen as a life-long thing. Now, 70% of people live together before getting married, 40% of children born in Britain are born to people who aren't married, and almost half of marriages end in divorce. *Is there any point in getting married at all?!*
>
> So today we're starting in Genesis 2, at the start of the story of the human race, when the first humans were living in God's perfect world.

A THE BLUEPRINT   Read Genesis 2 v 21-25

1 What relationship did God design man and woman to have (v 24)?

2 What does verse 25 tell us about what this couple's relationship was like?

Unlike in this scene, today all husbands and wives are sinners. There is no such thing as a perfect marriage. You may have been close to marriages which seemed perfect, or to marriages which caused lots of pain. Or perhaps the people closest to you aren't married at all. But it's worth remembering that God invented marriage: He made it to be great, and He says it's a good thing.

B PICTURE THIS

3 Of all the places you've been in this country (or even in the world), what's your favourite place? Why might it be nice to have a picture of that place in your bedroom?

4 Would the picture be worth anything itself? Would the picture be as good as the actual place?

C · HUSBAND: A HARD JOB

Read Ephesians 5 v 21-33

5 Husbands are meant to love their wives! What example does a husband need to follow to truly love his wife?

6 This is worth repeating. Because Christ loved His followers ("the church"), what did He do for them?

7 So how far should a husband be willing to go for his wife? What do you think this will mean for day-to-day life as a husband?

D · A REALLY GORGEOUS WIFE

8 Christ gave everything He had to His people so that the church would become what (v 26-27)?

We'd all love to have a wife who is "radiant", who never gets any wrinkles, and who has no imperfections or blemishes... she'd look gorgeous! And verse 28 tells husbands to love their wives "in the same way"—helping them be truly beautiful.

9 But look at verse 27. What is the opposite of being a "wrinkly" wife?

10 So what kind of "beauty" should be most important to a man as he thinks about getting married? What sort of beauty should a husband be helping his wife to achieve?

In other words, to take one example, it's much more important that a husband prays with his wife than that he buys her nice clothes.

E   A BIT ABOUT WIVES

You'll have noticed that Paul isn't only talking to Christian men here—he also has something to say to Christian women, in verses 22-24. "Wives should submit to their husbands in everything" (v 24).

To "submit" doesn't mean to blindly obey or to be a doormat! It means to allow the husband to take the lead, to take responsibility for making tough decisions, to be loyal and supportive of the husband—just as the church should be loyal and supportive to Christ, and should allow Christ to take the lead in its life.

So a Christian wife's submission to her husband is a picture of the church's relationship with Jesus.

Let's take a breath and think about where we've got to!
Marriage is a picture: a portrait of Christ's relationship with His people.

Think about what we've seen in Genesis 2 and Ephesians 5.

⓫ What is different here from how people in society think of sex, marriage and being a husband or wife?

⓬ How do these passages shape our thinking:
if we're thinking about proposing to a girl (think about what being a Christian husband involves)?

if we're considering asking someone out?

To think more about the whole area of going out with someone, have a look at "What about dating?" on page 66.

PRAYER TIME

Why not use the STOP system to help you speak to God together?

Sorry for...

Thank you for...

Others I'd like to pray for...

Please help me with...

MEMORY VERSE

"Love your wives, JUST AS CHRIST LOVED the church and gave himself up for her."   *Ephesians 5 v 25*

Session 12 A family man Solo

Today's Bible section: Ephesians 6 v 1-9

> In the last chunk of Ephesians you looked at, as Paul started to talk about marriage, he was also starting a longer section on how following Christ affects our relationships: in marriage, with parents and at work.

A OH, BUT MUM...

1 When do you find it difficult to do what one of your parents tells you? (You can be honest, no one else is going to see this!)

2 Why do you find it difficult to obey in those situations?

Today you'll be looking at the difficult issue of how to relate to your parents. Perhaps you get along well with your parents—or maybe you don't, and perhaps that's not at all your fault.

But whatever kind of relationship we have with our parents, God wants us to live as His people in how we treat them. *So, before you dig into the Bible, ask God to teach you and change you in this tricky area.*

Read Ephesians 6 v 1-4.

A useful definition of "children" (v 1) is people who live with, and rely financially on, their parents.

3 What should children do (v 1)?

4 What is the benefit of following God's word in this area (v 3)?

Verse 3 doesn't necessarily mean that God will add years to your life each time you obey your parents! But if families treat each other as

52

Ephesians 6 v 1-4 says, then that will strengthen families, which will lead to a stable, secure society, which in turn tends to lead to people being happier and living longer. Simple, huh?!

Paul reminds us in verse 2 that "Honour your father and mother" is one of the Ten Commandments (you can read them in Exodus 20 v 1-17). We've seen that while you're living at home, honouring your parents means obeying them.

5 How do you think Christian men can honour their parents once they've left home and are financially independent?

B WHO'S A DADDY?

6 What are Christian guys who are fathers told to do (v 4)?

Not to...

But to...

It's worth noticing that Paul has something to say about how Christian parents should behave, as well as how Christian children should behave. It just so happens that at the moment, you are probably a son, but not yet a father!

SCENARIOS

For each of these scenarios, write down how you might be *tempted* to react, and how a young Christian man *should* react, when one of his parents says...

"Please wash the dishes—and do it properly; make sure you don't leave bits of grease on the pans."

"You're not going out because you haven't done your homework."

"You've watched enough TV in your bedroom today already. While I'm out, I'd like you to keep it switched off."

"I don't care if you've done all your work and chores, I have just decided that you are not seeing your friends this weekend."

"There's no God, so there's no point in talking to Him. So I don't want you to waste time on praying." (Be careful with this one—Christian children should "obey your parents *in the Lord*" ie: put obeying God first.)

If you're unsure about any of these, make sure you mention them in your next joint session.

C   A WORD ABOUT WORK   Read verses 5-9

This section is talking about the relationship between slaves and masters. Slaves are to remember they're not just working for their master but for God Himself, and masters need to remember that they also have a Master in heaven (v 9) and so they should treat their slaves as their own Master, God, treats them.

We're unlikely (hopefully!) ever to be slaves; but you may have a Saturday job, or a paper round, or be leaving school soon to start working full-time. And in our work we need to remember as Christian guys that we're not just working for our boss but also for God. God invented work (it was part of His perfect creation), so He wants us to work well.

And if we're ever someone's boss, we'll need to work hard at treating them as God treats us—with love and fairness.

7 What is the main thing I need to change in my thinking or behaviour from this Bible section?

8 When I'm next tempted to disobey my parents, what am I going to think to myself? What positive action can I take?

PRAYER TIME

Write a short prayer based on this passage. Remember both to thank God and to ask Him for help in following Him. Try to be specific, talking to Him about the details of your own life and feelings.

A man of war Joint

Today's Bible section: Ephesians 6 v 10-20

A ACTION MOVIE

❶ Why do guys often like films about war? How do we tend to feel about the hero?

As we read this section, we'll discover that men were made to fight in a war! It turns out God made you to be a man of battle.

B THE FIGHT OF YOUR LIFE   Read Ephesians 6 v 10-20

❷ What idea is repeated in v 10, 11, 13 and 14?

❸ Who do we need to stand against (v 11-12)?

❹ What do you think he is aiming to do to Christians?

❺ Who is in this battle against him?

Look back at 2 v 2 (we looked at it a long time ago!) There the devil is described as "the spirit who is at work in those who are disobedient". Basically, everyone is either fighting the devil or has lost to the devil. Christians are people who fight.

C YOUR EQUIPMENT

❻ What do Christians need to do in order to stand and resist the devil (v 11)?

7 This is a spiritual battle, so the equipment is going to be spiritual too. Use verses 14-17 to label the gear on this spiritual warrior. For each one, think about why this is a great bit of spiritual equipment.

8 There's another weapon that Christians have as they stand and battle the devil. What is it (v 18)?

9 Why is this such a powerful weapon? (Tip—look back to 3 v 20 for help.)

10 And there's one final weapon... what does Paul ask his Christian friends to pray he'd be able to do (v19-20)?

Telling people the good news about Jesus (the "gospel") is taking the fight to the devil. What the devil hates most is people starting to follow Jesus—and the more we tell people about Jesus, the more chances people have to start following Him. Talking about Jesus is a great attacking weapon for us to use against the devil, just as it was for Paul!

Paul tells us in verse 20 that he is "in chains" in prison for being a Christian. Physically, Paul is losing the battle against people who don't love Jesus; but spiritually he isn't, because he's still standing and fighting the devil—and that's what matters most. When we lose out on things, or when people laugh at us because we're a Christian, we need to remember that it's the spiritual battle that really counts. Better to be in chains than to stop standing firm against the devil.

D THINK ABOUT IT

11 How does this section affect the way we should think about...

what is happening when we are tempted (use v 16 to help you)?

what we should do when we're tempted?

12 Write down one or two areas of your life where you know you are facing a battle to stand your ground and keep living God's way.

13 Do you pray verses 19-20 for yourself, and for your Christian friends? Look at what Paul talks about there. Why is it a good thing to "make known ... the gospel"? Why do we often try to avoid doing it?

14 How does this Bible section encourage you?

How does this Bible section challenge you?

PRAYER TIME

Prayer is a brilliant weapon (v 18). Use it now as you talk to God openly and honestly, either out loud or in your head. Write a prayer about the areas where you know you need to battle the devil.

"Put on the full armour of God so that you can TAKE YOUR STAND against the devil's schemes."
Ephesians 6 v 11

E THE LAST JOINT BIT (SOB!)

This is the end of your last joint session... why not spend a couple of minutes telling each other how you've been encouraged by your times together... how you've been challenged by what you've read in Ephesians... and what you'd like prayer for in the coming weeks and months.

Session 14 A real man Solo

Today's Bible section: Ephesians 6 v 21-24

Don't forget to pray that God would help you understand what He's saying and that it would make a difference to your life.

A PAUL'S POSTMAN   Read Ephesians 6 v 21-24

As you answer the questions, remember to use your own words wherever you can!

❶ Remember that Paul's locked up in prison. Who is Paul going to use to take this letter to Ephesus (v 21)? How does Paul describe him (v 21)?

❷ Why was he sending him to the Ephesian Christians (v 21-22)?

Paul's letters are sprinkled with reminders that he was a normal guy, just like us. He had been given a special job by God, but he was a real man, living in the real world. People like him and Tychicus faced the same kind of struggles as we do (and sometimes a lot worse, like being imprisoned).

❸ Tricky question... This letter is about what a Christian is, and how a Christian should live. Why do you think it's important to remember the man who wrote this was a real, living, breathing guy, just like us?

B IF YOU REMEMBER ONE THING...   Re-read verse 24

❹ Re-read verse 24. What does Paul remind his friends that they have, if they love Jesus properly?

❺ What does "grace" mean?

❻ Look back through the letter. What has God, in His undeserved kindness, done for us, or given us?

2 v 5:   1 v 13-14:

4 v 7, 11-12 (this one's trickier!):   6 v 11:

Paul was a real man who really lived the adventure of following Christ. Sometimes this made his life really hard; but he knew that living for Jesus was how a real man lives. He knew that God had given him everything he needed to live for Christ each day. And he knew that God had given him perfect eternal life with Jesus.

Verses 21-24 remind us that all we've learned from Ephesians isn't just meant to sit in our heads, like knowing some mathematical equation or chemical symbols; it's meant to make a difference to our lives as we get on with the adventure of being real men, men who follow Christ.

PRAYER TIME

One encouragement to give thanks for:

One challenge to pray about:

MEMORY VERSE

"GRACE to all who love our Lord Jesus Christ with an undying love." *Ephesians 6 v 24*

D THE END (NEARLY)

7 Make the time to sit down for thirty minutes and read the whole letter (after all, letters are meant to be read all in one go, even though we tend to split them into little chunks!) As you read it, write down...

Great things about Jesus...

Great things about following Jesus...

Things that you've found out you need to start doing, stop doing or do more of in order to follow Jesus better...

8 In one or two sentences, write down the big thing you're going to take away from Ephesians...

E THE END (REALLY)

You've finished your time in Ephesians, and you've finished this Real Men 121 booklet! But you don't need to stop there. Here are a couple of suggestions for how you can keep digging into God's word and keep growing as a real man:

ENGAGE daily Bible-reading notes

Helps you see what God has to say about Himself, and about you. As well as working through books of the Bible, Engage is stacked full of articles focussing on particular issues and real-life stories.
Grab a copy at: www.thegoodbook.co.uk/teenagers/
bible-reading/engage (UK)
www.thegoodbook.com/teenagers/
devotionals (US)

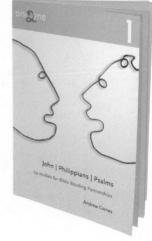

ONE2ONE for reading the Bible together

Keep exploring God's word together with these simple, easy-to-use one2one Bible-reading notes.
Grab a copy at: www.thegoodbook.co.uk/one2one (UK)
www.thegoodbook.com/one2one (US)

PUT OFF your **old self**, which is being corrupted...

...PUT ON the **new self**, created to be like God

Ephesians 4 v 22, 24

Ephesians 5 v 21-33 (Session 11) is all about marriage. But let's face it, you're probably not thinking about getting married yet. The whole issue of going out with girls is probably more relevant to your life right now.

While the Bible has a lot to say about marriage, it has little to say about dating (which should remind us that God thinks marriage is far more important a relationship than simply "being with someone").

BIBLE WISDOM. There are areas of life in which the Bible doesn't give us a direct command. You'll never open it up and find a verse saying "Go out with Michelle—she's gorgeous"! But it does offer us some wisdom which we can apply to our lives—and who to go out with is something we need to be wise about.

There's often great pressure on teenage guys to go out with someone (or at least get physical with someone, but re-read 5 v 3). But God tells us it's wise as Christian guys to be careful who we decide to go out with. And there's one story in the Old Testament that's very helpful...

SETTING THE SCENE. Here's what's going on. In those days (3,000 years ago) God's followers all lived together in one country, called Israel. And God had chosen one of His followers, Solomon, to be their king, and told him to lead them and help them follow God properly, so they could, in the words of Ephesians: "Live a life worthy of the calling you have received" (4 v 1). And Solomon had been great at following God and helping others to follow God, until...

> ¹King Solomon, however, loved many foreign women besides Pharaoh's daughter [who was Solomon's first wife]—Moabites, Ammonites, Edomites, Sidonians and Hittites. ²They were from nations about which the LORD had told the Israelites, "You must not intermarry with them, because they will surely turn your hearts after their gods." Nevertheless, Solomon held fast to them in love. ³He had seven hundred wives of royal birth and three hundred concubines [live-in lovers], and his wives led him astray. ⁴As Solomon grew old, his wives turned his heart after other gods, and his heart was not fully devoted to the LORD his God, as the heart of David his father had been. ⁵He

followed Ashtoreth the goddess of the Sidonians, and Molech the detestable god of the Ammonites. ⁶So Solomon did evil in the eyes of the Lord; he did not follow the Lord completely, as David his father had done.

⁷On a hill east of Jerusalem, Solomon built a high place for Chemosh the detestable god of Moab, and for Molech the detestable god of the Ammonites. ⁸He did the same for all his foreign wives, who burned incense and offered sacrifices to their gods.

⁹The Lord became angry with Solomon because his heart had turned away from the Lord, the God of Israel, who had appeared to him twice. ¹⁰Although he had forbidden Solomon to follow other gods, Solomon did not keep the Lord's command. ¹¹So the Lord said to Solomon, "Since this is your attitude and you have not kept my covenant and my decrees, which I commanded you, I will most certainly tear the kingdom away from you and give it to one of your subordinates."

1 Kings 11:1-11

WIFE WARNING. Solomon had been warned (v 2) not to marry "foreign" women—in other words, women who weren't part of God's people. This wasn't because God ("the Lord") thought foreign women were ugly, or boring, or not as good as Israelite women. It was because He knew that having a relationship with a woman who didn't follow God would sooner or later make it virtually impossible for a guy to keep following God.

But Solomon didn't listen—he "loved many foreign women" (v 1). In fact, he had seven hundred wives and three hundred concubines (sort of unofficial wives, v 3). He must have been a very busy man—imagine trying to keep 700 wives (and 300 lovers) happy!

But what mattered most was not *how many* wives Solomon had, but *who they worshipped*. And sure enough, just as God had warned, Solomon's wives "turned his heart after other gods, and his heart was not fully devoted to the Lord his God" (v 4). Because Solomon's wives followed other ways of life and not the way of life God wanted, Solomon ended up not following God and just doing what his wives did.

Look at how God reacted (v 9): "The Lord became angry with Solomon because his heart had turned away from the Lord". From the dizzying heights of being God's number one guy, His right-hand man, Solomon ended up as low as you can get—with God being angry with him.

CHOOSE CAREFULLY. This story acts as a warning to God's people today. The person you choose to have a close relationship with, be it as a girlfriend now or a wife in the future, will have a huge influence over what you believe and how you act. It's hard enough following Christ each day without having someone you love encouraging you not to bother!

So the Bible's wise advice is: "Don't do a Solomon"—don't go out with girls who may be good-looking and really fun, but who don't follow Christ. Remember that your relationship with Jesus is the only one which gives you eternal life—no girl offers anything as good as that. Remember that the priority in finding a girl is that she's someone who follows Jesus, and who you can team up with to encourage each other in living God's way. And, of course, if she's good-looking and fun to be with, then that's great too!

Bit Extra **What about homosexuality?** Read

Ephesians 5 v 21-33 (Session 11) is all about marriage between a man and a woman. What about relationships between two people of the same sex? What does God say in the Bible about homosexuality?

SEX IS GOOD. God invented it (Genesis 2 v 24-25)! And since He invented it, He knows how it should be used and enjoyed—and He says it's to be used within a marriage between a man and a women. Jesus Himself underlined this point during His life on earth (Mark 10 v 6-9).

SEX CAN BE MISUSED. This means that ALL sex outside heterosexual marriage goes against God's good plans. Sex before marriage, adultery, and homosexual sex are all ways of disobeying God, and leave us facing His right anger at our rebellion (remember Ephesians 2 v 1-3?) The Bible says homosexual sex *is* a sin. But we also need to realise it's *no worse* than any other sin. We all struggle with sin—some people struggle with homosexual feelings, others with anger, others with envy, for example.

GOD LOVES ALL PEOPLE. Sometimes you see people holding placards saying "God hates gays", as if God has a special category of hatred for homosexual people. But God hates all sin—and, amazingly, He loves all sinners enough to have come to earth in the person of Jesus and died on the cross so He can offer people forgiveness (Romans 5 v 8).

GOD CHANGES HIS PEOPLE. Through Jesus' death we can be forgiven, and through the Holy Spirit's work in us we can be helped to resist sinning, and changed to be more like Jesus. Paul wrote a letter to a different church, in which he says that sin, including homosexual sex, leaves us outside God's eternal kingdom: "And that is what some of you were. But you were washed, you were sanctified [ie: made pure], you were justified [ie: found not guilty] in the name of the Lord Jesus Christ and by the Spirit of our God" (1 Corinthians 6 v 11).

GOD'S WAY IS NOT EASY. We've seen that living as a follower of Jesus means we "must no longer live as the Gentiles do"—we're not to be guided simply by what "feels" right, by sensuality (Ephesians 4 v 17, 19). Jesus said anyone who followed Him must "deny himself" (Mark 8 v 34). That means sometimes our mind and body will be telling us to do something, but we say "no"—we deny ourselves in order to obey God. If you or a Christian friend are tempted by homosexual sex, that will mean saying "no" to what your mind and body want to do. If you're tempted by heterosexual sex outside marriage, or by anger, gossip, selfishness, or any other sin, it will mean saying "no" to those things. God never said living His way, following His Son, would be easy, but...

GOD'S WAY IS WORTH IT. God knows what's best for us—He made us! And living with Him in charge means we can look forward to "our inheritance", perfect life in His eternal kingdom (Ephesians 1 v 14). There, we won't struggle with temptation any more, and we won't sin any more. We'll enjoy perfect life, just as God created us to do. So, if you or a Christian friend are struggling with homosexual temptation, remember where you're headed—to perfect life with your amazing God. Life there is better than anything you can experience in life now. So say "no" to sin... if you do sin, know that you can be forgiven... and be excited about your future perfect life with Jesus.

There is much more to say about this—you might have questions or worries. If you do (or if a friend does), a great thing to do is talk to an older Christian you can trust. Or if you'd rather, there are Christian organisations that can help. Make sure they are seeking to obey what the Bible says. A good place to start in the UK is: www.truefeedomtrust.co.uk

To help you tell your friends about Jesus...
www.christianityexplored.org

The Christianity Explored website is like a toolbox, equipping you to talk to people you know about Jesus. And you can point your friends to it too, so that they can keep finding out more about Christianity themselves. It features:

- answers to tough questions
- a visual outline explaining what Christianity is
- real life stories of people's experiences of becoming Christians.

Why not take a look?

To help show your friends who Jesus is...
one2one: Just Looking

If you know someone who's really interested in what you believe, the best thing you can do is get them reading God's word!

That's what one of the books in this one2one range is designed to do. *Just Looking* makes it easy for you and a friend to look at the Gospel of Luke in the New Testament, so that they, and you, can come face to face with Jesus, and discover who He is, why He came, and why He matters to all of us.

You can order a copy (or two) here: www.thegoodbook.co.uk/ one2one-just-looking (UK) www.thegoodbook.com/ one2one-just-looking (US)

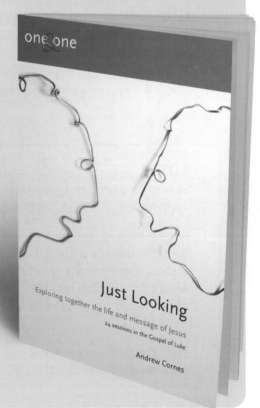

thegoodbook
COMPANY

At The Good Book Company, we are dedicated to helping Christians and local churches grow. We believe that God's growth process always starts with hearing clearly what He has said to us through His timeless word—the Bible.

Ever since we opened our doors in 1991, we have been striving to produce resources that honour God in the way the Bible is used. We have grown to become an international provider of user-friendly resources to the Christian community, with believers of all backgrounds and denominations using our Bible studies, books, resources for those wanting to find out about the Christian faith, DVD-based courses and training events.

We want to equip ordinary Christians to live for Christ day by day, help churches to grow in their knowledge of God and their love for one another, and enable people to explore the Christian message and think it through for themselves. Call us for a discussion of your needs, or visit one of our websites for more information on the resources and services we provide, and how to obtain our materials throughout the world.

UK & Europe: www.thegoodbook.co.uk
N America: www.thegoodbook.com
Australia: www.thegoodbook.com.au
New Zealand: www.thegoodbook.co.nz

Tel UK: 0345 225 0880
Tel International: +44 (0) 208 942 0880

LOST
When the dream turns to a nightmare

A great book to read yourself and then give away to a friend. LOST is short, funny and uses a parable Jesus told to explain why He came, and why all of us need to know Him.

www.thegoodbook.co.uk/lost
www.thegoodbook.com/lost

LOST
When the Dream turns
to a Nightmare

Jonty Allcock